STRATHCLYDE UNIVERSITY LIBRARY

30125 00395922 7

D1140600

ANDERSON'S LIBRARY
✱
WITHDRAWN
FROM
LIBRARY
STOCK
✱
UNIVERSITY OF STRATHCLYDE

7

SIR JAMES GOWANS

Romantic Rationalist

Books are to be returned on or before
the last date below.

94006

SIR JAMES GOWANS

Romantic Rationalist

DUNCAN McARA

ANDERSONIAN LIBRARY

5. MAR 91

UNIVERSITY OF STRATHCLYDE

Paul Harris Publishing

1975

UNIVERSITY OF
STRATHCLYDE LIBRARIES

First published 1975,
European Architectural Heritage Year, by
PAUL HARRIS PUBLISHING,
50 Montrose Terrace, Edinburgh.

International Standard Book Number 0 904505 00 6.

© Duncan McAra 1975.

To my father and mother

This Edition limited to 750 copies
of which this is Number ....

ANDERSONIAN LIBRARY

0 5. MAR 91

UNIVERSITY OF STRATHCLYDE

This book is published with the assistance of the
Scottish Arts Council.

Printed by the Shetland Times Ltd., Lerwick, Shetland.

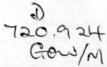

CONTENTS

ILLUSTRATIONS

PREFACE

Of the many nineteenth and early twentieth-century buildings which I have visited in the British Isles, there are a few which have left a lasting impression: Rockville and the Barclay Church in Edinburgh; Sir John Soane's Museum in London; Lissadell, near Sligo; the former St. Vincent Street Church and the Glasgow School of Art. Modern buildings which have exerted a similar fascination include the Nuffield Transplantation Surgery Unit, Edinburgh; St. Benedict's RC Church, Glasgow; and the Department of Engineering, University of Leicester.

These buildings compel the student of architecture to visit them again and again in order that their vital complexity and taut passion be fully understood and appreciated. It is the first mentioned of these buildings, Rockville, which forms the heart of this short book — the result of an interest dating from 1965.

I should like to thank each of the following, who in some specific way offered advice or assistance during the preparation of this book: Mr Alexander Bain, Miss Catherine Cruft, Mr James C. Haggart, Miss Agnes Harrison, Mr Edwin Johnston, Mrs Isabel McLean, Mr Colin McWilliam, Dr David C. Simpson, Mr David Walker, and the staffs of the Edinburgh Room and the Fine Art Room in Edinburgh Central Public Library.

Photographs were provided by the author (plates 2, 3, 14, 15, 17, 18), Edinburgh City Archivist (plate 1), Edinburgh City Museums (plate 22), Mr James C. Haggart (plate 8), Mr Edwin Johnston (plates 9, 10, 11) and the Royal Commission on the Ancient & Historical Monuments of Scotland (plates 5, 6, 7, 12, 13, 16, 19, 20, 21).

PART ONE : 1821 - 1857

'The great problems of modern construction must have a geometric solution.' (Le Corbusier)

Every great architect has his own unmistakable idiom — his hallmark and vocabulary by which he is recognised and understood. This is true of renowned figures ranging from Robert Adam, Claude-Nicolas Ledoux and Sir John Soane to Antoni Gaudí, Charles Rennie Mackintosh and Louis Kahn. If a similar claim to eminence is presented here for the nineteenth-century Scottish architect and engineer Sir James Gowans, it is because in his own idiosyncratic way he, too, had an expressive and complex vocabulary.

The essential importance of Sir James Gowans is this: that in the relative isolation of Edinburgh during the 1850s and '60s, he designed buildings, based on a consistent theory, which were a signpost in one of the several directions architectural theory was later to take. This is best shown by his romantic, polychromatic, but basically rational buildings which display Gowans's rigorous adherence to a 2 ft module and fixed angles to facilitate standardisation and economic mass-production of stone building-components.

It was the combination of his inventiveness of design, skilful use of materials, strong colour-sense and preoccupation with quality and perfection of details which has made Sir James Gowans not only one of the most important of Scotland's architects but one of the most original European master-builders of the nineteenth century.

James Gowans was born in Blackness — a village some fifteen miles north-west of Edinburgh on the shore of the Forth — on 1 August 1821, the third son of Walter and Isabella

B

Gowans. Walter Gowans, a local mason, was born in 1789 and his wife (*née* de Grotte) in 1790. The family's gravestone in the parish churchyard at Torphichen, West Lothian, bears tragic evidence of the social conditions prevalent in Great Britain in the early nineteenth century: John Gowans, 1819-24; Andrew Gowans, 1824-40; John Gowans, 1829-56; Mary Gowans, 1836-58.

Although there is no record of the causes of the first two premature deaths, it is not unlikely that they were, as in the case of the younger John Gowans, a result of 'disease of the heart' or else, phthisis or smallpox.

Blackness was situated a mere twelve miles from the scene near Carron when, in 1820, the authorities were confronted with riots similar to earlier Radical agitation at Spa Fields in London (1816) and St. Peter's Fields in Manchester (1819). Sir Walter Scott wrote disparagingly of this unrest: 'The whole Radical plot went to the devil, when it came to blood and sword. Scarce any blood was shed, except in a trifling skirmish at Bonnymuir, near Carron.'

Despite widespread agricultural and industrial distress, there was still a pleasant aspect of the Scottish Lowlands: before the advent of railways, coalmining and light industries, such as brewing and printing, the landscape of the Lothians, Fife and the Borders was completely rural and the beauty of Edinburgh's surrounding countryside during the early years of James Gowans's life was conveyed by several painters, e.g. Alexander Nasmyth, J. W. Ewbank, John Thomson, Alexander Carse and David Octavius Hill (later to become famous as a calotype photographer).

About this period, Walter Gowans bought some property, known locally as Andrew's Yards, situated about six miles south-west of Linlithgow. For a short time the Gowans family lived there in the house, subsequently enlarged by James Gowans and known appropriately as Gowanbank.

In 1833, Walter Gowans left West Lothian and moved his family to the village of Stockbridge, then on the outskirts of Edinburgh. They lived at 25 Dean Street and Walter Gowans entered the city's building trade. The main reason for Gowans's move to Edinburgh was financial. He had clearly realised that this elegant and prosperous city was only on the threshold of expansion and development, in which an experienced builder could participate to his own financial gain. Although the first step had been taken over sixty years previously with the planning and construction of the early New Town and the North and South Bridges, it was only the beginning.

As Edinburgh's population increased from 162,000 in 1830 to 270,000 by 1890, the city's boundaries spread farther and farther outwards, chiefly to the south and west.

During the period between Waterloo and the accession of Queen Victoria, two of the most important additions to the city were its new bridges. The first of these — the Regent Bridge (1815) — enabled Waterloo Place to be cut ruthlessly through the Old Calton Burial Ground and open up a direct approach to Princes Street from the east. J. M. W. Turner has left a contemporary illustration, *Edinburgh from Calton Hill* (engraved by G. Cooke, 1820), in which great attention has been given to the erection of the Regent Bridge and the masons, dressing the stones in their 'lodges' or workshops.

This, in turn, led to the development of impressive terraces on the shoulders of Calton Hill — Regent, Carlton and Royal Terraces. These houses, begun in 1819 by W. H. Playfair (1789-1857), had access to private gardens on Calton Hill laid out by Sir Joseph Paxton (1801-65). Thomas Hamilton (1784-1858) was appointed by the Town Council to design on the southern slope of Calton Hill the Royal High School, a Grecian Doric masterpiece of Craigleith stone, which has since been described by Sir John Summerson as 'the noblest monument of the Scottish Greek Revival.'[1]

Similar developments also took place to the west of the city where the Water of Leith flows through a deep gorge. In 1832, Thomas Telford (1757-1834) constructed the magnificently slender Dean Bridge, which thus facilitated north-west expansion and offered easy access from the city to the passage across the Forth at South Queensferry.

Perhaps it is all the more difficult then to understand Lord

Cockburn's strictures of the New Town of Edinburgh, the conservation of which is guided and advanced so vigorously at the
present day by the Cockburn Association, the Scottish Georgian
Society and the Scottish Civic Trust in collaboration with
Edinburgh Corporation: 'What a site did nature give us for
our New Town! Yet what insignificance in its plan! What
poverty in all its details! . . . Our jealousy of variety, and our
association of magnificence with sameness, was really curious.
If builders ever attempted to deviate so far from the established
paltriness as to carry up the front wall so as to hide the
projecting slates, or to break the roof by a Flemish storm-
window, or to turn the gable to the street, there was an immediate outcry.'[2] These views, of course, were largely coloured
by a visit he made in 1823 to the Continent, where he admired,
in particular, the picturesque streets and irregular rooflines of
Flemish, Italian and Swiss towns.

    To Ruskin's eye, Georgian Edinburgh was 'nothing but
square cut stone — square cut stone — a wilderness of square
cut stone for ever and for ever'.[3] And to return to Lord Cockburn: 'In towns, the great modern object has uniformly been to
extinguish all picturesque relics of antiquity and to reduce
everything to the dullest and baldest uniformity.'[4]

    At the beginning of Victoria's reign, James Gowans left
Hamilton Place Academy in Stockbridge and entered the emer-
gent architectural profession. (The Institute of British Architects
— later RIBA — was founded in London in 1834; the
Architectural Institute of Scotland — later RIAS — began in
1840.) Like most cities nowadays, Edinburgh offers courses in
architecture, town planning and building at its universities and
colleges. In 1837, on the other hand, no such facilities existed.

    In a paper read many years later in 1883, James Gowans
explained the position of a student in his own youth: 'When I
first remember, there were in the city many drawing classes,
chiefly attended by young men who were either masons, car-
penters, engineers or mechanics. There was Ruthven on the
Bridges, Milne in St. James's Square, Moffat of George Street

and Paterson of Stockbridge, and others, all teaching drawing and making good incomes from the crowded classes that attended them. Besides this, there was at every important building a drawing class, usually conducted by the chief foreman or clerk of works, which had the effect of theoretically educating the workman to a proficiency he could not otherwise have attained.'[5]

Despite the impact of Pugin's notorious pleas for Catholicism and Gothic archictecture in *Contrasts* (1836) and *True Principles of Pointed or Christian Architecture* (1841), Georgian architecture did not suddenly come to a halt. When James Gowans was training to become an architect in the George Street office of David Bryce (1803-76), a man later to become a Scottish Baronial expert, the Classical influence was still felt and widely appreciated and was to flourish well into the 1850s and '60s. In *Style and Society* (1971), Robert Macleod commented: 'It was slightly easier to do this [defend the use of Classical precedent] in Scotland than in England. There was, first of all, a stronger Reformation tradition which tended to shy away from anything implicitly Catholic in its associations. . . . It could perhaps be argued that there was in the national character a greater attachment to the rational and to intellectual discipline than to the empirical and the emotive.[6] Collectively, it is not difficult to see why the Gothic Revival made far fewer inroads into Scottish architecture during the nineteenth century than it did in England.'[7]

Towards the end of the 1840s there developed an aspect of Classical architecture, known as Graeco-Roman, the influence of which was strongest among Scottish banks. In 1847, what was to become the finest example of this particular style was the head office of the Commercial Bank of Scotland (now incorporated into the Royal Bank of Scotland), designed by David Rhind (1808-83). It was built at the eastern end on the south side of George Street in Edinburgh and the firm responsible for the construction of this masterpiece in stone from Binny Quarry, West Lothian, was Walter Gowans & Sons.

In 1846, James Gowans temporarily turned aside from

architecture and gave his attention to railway engineering as offering a wider scope for his energy, capabilities and financial advancement. Indeed, it's not difficult to understand his sudden desire to participate in the 'railway mania'.

Only two years previously, in 1844, J. M. W. Turner had exhibited in the Royal Academy an oil painting entitled *Rain, Steam and Speed — the Great Western Railway*.[8] In this work an early locomotive was shown against a misty landscape charging across a bridge sweating steam and fiery sparks. The sheer intensity of mechanical speed experienced by Turner and conveyed in paint symbolised a revolution which was soon to transform the appearance of the British landscape, the organisation of heavy industry and commerce and the public's social habits.

In contrast to the short-sighted railway closures of the present day, the 1840s and '50s witnessed the growth of a vast network of railways, branch lines and railway centres.

In Edinburgh the most visible symbol of the gulf which separated Gowans, Bryce and Rhind from Adam, Mylne and Craig was the railway through Princes Street Gardens.

Railways of a kind had been in existence long before George Stephenson's Stockton and Darlington Railway (1825) or the Liverpool and Manchester (1830). On many English estates, for instance, a system of wooden rails had been used to carry trucks (often horse-drawn) from collieries and other mines to depots beside rivers and canals for transportation. The construction of railways in southern Scotland had been in progress, too, for a number of years before Gowans was appointed an engineer. The Edinburgh and Dalkeith line was opened in 1831 and, by 1842, Edinburgh and Glasgow were linked at a cost of just over £1 million; this was one of the early railways, the track of which was supported by large square blocks of stone, before the introduction of wooden sleepers.

Sir J. H. A. MacDonald, a former Lord Justice-Clerk of the Court of Session of Scotland, has given an amusing account of the transition from horse-drawn coaches to rail travel: 'Even when it was seen to be more sensible to make carriages for the railroad longer and closed-in, the mail-coach idea did not altogether lose its hold on the designer. The three compartments of a carriage had their sides made to bulge out in curves similar to the lines of the old mail-coach. The guard was, as he had been on the mail-coach, perched upon the top. And as the luggage had been piled on the roof of the mail-coach, so the luggage was put on top of the railway carriages.'[9] This particular detail was recorded by William Frith in his painting *The Railway Station* (1862), now hanging in Royal Holloway College near Windsor.

Among the works accomplished by Gowans and his navvies were stretches of the Edinburgh and Bathgate Railway (1847), the Crieff branch line of the Caledonian Railway and the entire track from Edinburgh to North Berwick. His most important contract, however, was with the Highland Railway Company, for which he was responsible for the construction of such lines as those linking Dunkeld and Ballinluig, and Dalwhinnie to Boat o' Garten.

In the early 1850s, James Gowans left his house at Lynedoch Place and settled in 1 Randolph Cliff, looking out over the steep, tree-covered gorge of the Dean Valley.

While James Gowans had been occupied with railway engineering, his father had added quarrying to his business interests. In 1847, a lease had been granted by John Inglis of Redhall to Walter Gowans & Sons to work Redhall Quarry on the outskirts of Colinton, near the equally famous Hailes Quarry. Walter Gowans, whether through failing health or more important building commitments, soon became unable to manage the quarry, and in 1850 the lease was made over to James Gowans.

Dark red sandstone had been quarried in the district of Redhall at least as far back as 1650; the castle at Redhall, for example, had been built of this material. In 1757, the Inglis of Redhall had advertised a quarry for the supply of millstones 'of exceeding good quality' up to 5 ft in diameter. A later advertisement in 1781 stated: 'The excellent good qualities of this stone both for hewn and ornamental work is well known and has long been in great demand for the buildings in and about Edinburgh.' The particular attributes of this stone were its durability and colour, due mainly to its high content of silica. Stone from Redhall Quarry was used in Edinburgh for the building of houses in Heriot Row (1803-8), St. John's Episcopal Church (1816-18) and St. Paul's Episcopal Church (1816-18).

Gowans began by abandoning the traditional system of quarrying, which made use of wedges and small charges of gunpowder and, in its place, introduced at Redhall a method of rock-drilling by machines. Holes, usually of 3-4 in diameter were bored and then packed with explosive, ignited by a galvanic battery[10]. Gowans was not devoted solely, though, to the economics of quarry management. At this period in the nineteenth century, the public's imagination was stimulated by the discoveries made in geology and their possible consequences on biblical studies and current theological tenets.

In this particular area of science, one of Gowans's most famous contemporaries was Hugh Miller (1802-56), the Cromarty stonemason, whose geological observations caused him to publish such works as *The Old Red Sandstone* (1841), *Geology of the Bass Rock* (1848), *Testimony of the Rocks* (1857) and *The Cruise of the* Betsey (1859).

In 1855, an early French enthusiast for concrete, François Coignet, may have declared: 'Cement, concrete and iron are destined to replace stone'[11], but in Edinburgh such a remark would have been regarded not so much as near blasphemous but simply unnecessary and irrelevant. Because stone and masons were easily available, most Scottish architects built with stone, which also weathered well. As a mason's son, Gowans was fascinated by the tactile quality, textures and colours of different types of this natural and intrinsically beautiful material and by the discipline which this material imposed.

Gowans observed, for example, that in another of his quarries at Binny in West Lothian, many fissures were filled with bitumen some of which he collected and made into candles as a modest contribution to the 1851 Great Exhibition in London.

During these years of his life as a quarrymaster and engineer, James Gowans began to concern himself with the urgent problem of how best to house the growing number of working-class families in a city, whose development since 1830 had been directed largely at the extension of the New Town.

The paintings and sketches by Shepherd, Geikie, Drummond and Leitch often give a picturesque and theatrical impression of the narrow closes and wynds, which run rib-like off either side of the High Street. They presented, in fact, a rather misleading view of actual conditions in that area. The lack of development in the Old Town, together with the increasing density of population, caused the multi-storey stone tenements to be divided and subdivided into cramped accommodations, consisting very often of single rooms.

The census of 1861 revealed the startling facts that in Edinburgh 120 families lived in single rooms without any windows, and that 13,000 families lived in houses in single apartments. The sanitation of those dwellings was almost non-existent and, indeed, the scarcity of indoor lavatories in working-class houses was a defect common not only in Edinburgh and Glasgow, but throughout the country generally during the Victorian era.

The first glimmer of enlightenment in Victorian Edinburgh[12] occurred in 1841 with the founding of the Edinburgh Lodging-House Association, while eight years later, in 1849, a group of professional men formed the Pilrig Model Buildings Association with the intention of raising the standard of working-class accommodation. The Pilrig Model Buildings, designed by the architect Patrick Wilson, were erected off Leith Walk in 1850-1 at a cost of £6,800 and consisted of a scheme of forty-four houses in three two-storey blocks around a central court.

The urgency of the need to improve the quality of working-class housing was expounded frequently by the Earl of Shaftesbury and city medical officers and was officially recognised in 1851 at the Great Exhibition where Henry Roberts (1802-76) constructed Model Cottages with the full support of Prince Albert.

Three years after the Great Exhibition, Alexander Mac-Gregor was appointed to design the elevations of Rosebank Cottages — a compact scheme of thirty-six two-storey cottages in six blocks, opposite the curving tenement façade of Gardner's Crescent in Fountainbridge, Edinburgh. The internal design and construction were handled by James Gowans at a final cost of £8,000.

Each ground-floor flat was entered from a small garden; on the other side of each cottage, an external stair with Greek key-pattern cast-iron railings led up to a small balcony and the front doors of upper-floor flats. In a lecture delivered to members of the Architectural Institute of Scotland some years later, Gowans outlined the aims behind the design of these houses. They included an independent entrance to each flat; separate access to the bedrooms of parents and children; a w.c. and bath in the scullery of each house; locating the scullery in such a way as to simplify the problem of drainage; heating and ventilating each flat in a simple and efficient way.

Gowans also stated that instead of sealing the drains at the ends next to the closets, he had continued them by funnels up into the chimney-heads, from where foul air could easily be dispersed. His method of ventilation involved conveying fresh air into a 'receiving chamber' at the rear of each kitchen-grate and, after being heated, passing it through hollow bricks along the partitions and filtering it into different rooms by movable ventilators. The air was then carried by an 'extracting flue' in the ceiling up to the ridge of the roof and dispelled.

Because of the technical details to ensure that these cottages *were* habitable, functional and hygienic — not simply conscience-soothers for well-meaning social reformers — the rents were beyond the means of low-paid workers, and from the number of masons, builders, mechanics and clerks listed in the Street

Directory of that time, it is clear that Rosebank Cottages were occupied mainly by skilled artisans.

The most pleasing aspect of these houses was that they provided a degree of light, hygiene and privacy, unknown to the labouring class in the crowded, ill-lit, fetid warrens off the High Street. Many years later, when he was Edinburgh's Lord Dean of Guild, Gowans commented on Rosebank Cottages: 'The idea that I had was to get working men into small, self-contained houses, where they would have their own door to go in by, every room being independent of the others, having a door from the lobby for privacy, and having a little green attached to each house. For many years I gave a prize to those who kept the best garden and the best house, but that inducement failed.'[13]

As if to prove the sincerity of his concern for the welfare of the working man, Gowans was even prepared to leave his elegant West End address and live for the next four years at 34 Rosebank Cottage; it is more likely, however, that he was compelled for various financial reasons to reside, at least temporarily, in less expensive property.

Nevertheless, Gowans's genuine regard for the well-being of his quarry employees did lead him several years later, in 1857, to design and construct Redhall Bank Cottages (now 8 & 10 Redhall Bank Road) of local red sandstone from his own quarries. Both cottages consisted of ground floors with bedrooms and storage space left tucked under the steeply pitching roof.

John Ruskin's comment that 'the very soul of the cottage — the essence and meaning of it — are in its roof'[14] was certainly applicable to Gowans's cottages. Gowans's eye for an imaginative use of random stonework created a mosaic of rich colours from dark wasp-yellow to olive-grey and deep reddish-ochre. From the steep roof, Gowans brought out bedroom windows under deep-set, slate-covered hoods, while his taste for the picturesque showed itself in his extraordinary gabled chimneys, the effect of whose ornamental slats caused them to resemble square stone beehives. What is all the more revealing about Gowans's designs was his claim that the crazy-paving effect of his rubble-work was based on economic logic:

'In the country, where small houses suitable for agricultural labourers and others have to be provided and where economy in the use of material is the chief requirement, it is of the first consequence that the truthful application of the material be scrupulously attended to. When an architect is employed to design a building and furnish specifications, he too often adopts some favourite style of building and a stereotyped specification which, not being applicable to the district from which he has to get his material, involves a great and unnecessary expense; and in consequence, the building comes to too much money and to allow it to go on, the accommodation must be curtailed.'[15]

Redhall Bank Cottages were thus ideally situated in respect of the health and welfare of the quarriers and their families. Gowans enabled them to live in relative comfort and privacy in an environment free from the reeking haze of chimney smoke, which contributed to some degree certainly to the mortality rate in Victorian Edinburgh. They were built on a sheltered rise overlooking the Union Canal to the west and the Water of Leith to the east. This landscape, the tranquillity of which was disturbed only by quarry machinery and the distant thrashing of water from Boag's snuff-mill and Redhall flour-mill, made a deep impression on Robert Louis Stevenson when, as a child, he used to scramble down to the water's edge near Colinton Village to hear 'the moil of the mill' and watch 'the wonder of foam'.

The appearance of Gowans's early works already provides an indication that in architecture Gowans was not preoccupied with the 'style' of a building, such as the *cottage orné* or the Greek villa, but rather by economic considerations, the particular purpose of a building and its appearance in relation to its immediate surroundings. Gowans believed that before building 'what the architect had to look for primarily was a stone that was durable, strong and of a colour which would best bring out the architectural features of his design and harmonise with the locality and surroundings in which it was placed.'[16]

Gowans was not impervious, though, to the arguments put forward fiercely by his contemporaries on the subject of 'style'. He believed that 'in architecture a geometric basis is at the root of what we admire in the examples we have of the "True styles". If a new style of architecture is to be developed, we must fall back on what guided the old designers in their original conceptions of what was not only true to its use, true in construction, true in symmetry, but beautiful as well because *it was true* — the cube, circle and its geometric development giving that which we admire and call Classic, while the circle and the equilateral triangle supply the key to those noble Gothic structures which were erected five hundred years ago.'[17]

The Victorian obsession with 'truth', 'honesty' and 'propriety', expounded earnestly at great length by Ruskin in his *Seven Lamps of Architecture* (1849) and *Stones of Venice* (1851-3), had, of course, been first stimulated by the obtrusive publications of Pugin. Pugin had begun his *True Principles of Pointed or Christian Architecture* (1841) with 'the two great rules for design . . . that there should be no features about a building which are not necessary for convenience, construction, or propriety' and 'all ornament should consist of enrichment of the essential construction of the building.'

On the importance of good foundations, Gowans stressed his faith in rock, but where the strata were unequal or unreliable, he declared: 'I know of nothing better than a good bed of concrete, certainly not less that 3 ft thick . . . this is always necessary in erections of different heights, such as churches and other buildings where the spire, tower or other elevations bear more heavily on the foundations than the walls which abut them.'[18]

Gowans's experience as a quarrymaster enabled him to become a particularly well-qualified judge of the use and characteristics of stone as a building material: 'For one to know what *good* stone really is and know how it can be best used, the architect or student has not far to go to see not only the most durable stone, but also variety of masonry as exemplified in such buildings as Holyrood, Heriot's Hospital and the residential buildings of the Old Town, erected centuries ago; or turning to the modern buildings of the New Town, stone of equal durability and variety of masonry, as shown in the polished work of the better-class buildings of the terraces, crescents and squares, such as Royal Terrace, Randolph Crescent, Moray Place or Charlotte Square, while in George Square, Gilmore Place, Thistle Street, Rose Street or Jamaica Street, work of a cheaper kind has been adopted, all of which are not only instructive but interesting in showing what masons could do in erecting buildings that have stood the test of time, which makes no mistakes in exposing what is good or bad in the Art of Building.'[19]

A further topic which occupied Gowans was the variety of rubble masonry to be found throughout Edinburgh: 'Common rubble masonry or walls built with stones of irregular shape as they come from the quarries, if well put-together, well-dressed, well-knocked to their bed and built from front to back so as to bond, then enduring walls may be built. Another kind of rubble which was much in vogue when the houses in Moray Place, for instance, were built, as shown in the back walls and also in the front of the older houses in George Square and Gilmore Place, was that of Coursed Rubble. This work was done entirely with the piend hammer, without chisel marks of any kind. Where what is called Squared Rubble is adopted, the practice of running up the outer face should not be allowed; no worse masonry could be built than this and it is to be regretted that so much of this kind of work is being done in our city. For it is not only bad in itself, but leads to our younger masons being trained to a most objectionable style.'[20]

During the nineteenth century, the wide variety of rubble masonry such as common, squared, random, hammer-dressed, nidged and pick-dressed, along with speculation in building schemes gave rise to a noticeable unevenness in the standard of building.

During his life, James Gowans was aware of a gradual decline in the quality of masonry construction and realised that the main reason was that masons were not being trained properly, due to their being allowed to break their indentures and failing to serve their full time of apprenticeship.

'Masons were better trained when it was more the custom of indenturing apprentices for a term of years, usually five. Three years were devoted to the art of hewing and two to the art of building. When the term expired, it was usual for the master to attach a certificate to the indenture, stating how good an apprentice he had been and his qualification to take his place as a journeyman mason.'[21]

Gowans considered that it was a matter for serious regret that an architect's reputation should suffer on a building to which his design skill had been applied simply because of faulty stone or insufficient understanding of his material.

'Five hundred years ago, when those beautiful examples of Gothic architecture were erected with their traceried windows and vaulted roofs, the architect and builder seem to have gone hand-in-hand, not only in planning, but in building up edifices which have withstood the ravages of time for so long.'[22]

The explanation for this may be that the medieval mason acquired his skill and understanding of geometry by being apprenticed for a longer period, usually seven years. After his graduation, he worked as a mason for the next twenty years, gaining experience by hewing and building, until the day came when, as master-builder (Gk, *architekton*), full recognition was bestowed on him by his being given the responsibility of designing a building.

This deep absorption with the techniques of masonry construction caused Gowans to visit and study famous examples such as Edinburgh Castle, Holyrood Abbey, the Palace of Holyroodhouse, the post-Reformation architecture of the Old Town, Roslin Chapel and the Border Abbeys at Dryburgh, Jedburgh, Kelso and Melrose.

Gowans revealed a life-long interest in connection with this subject in a lecture given to members of the Edinburgh Architectural Association later in his career; this was his fascination with masons' marks:

'I wish to allude to a custom which prevailed when such buildings as Heriot's Hospital[23] were erected. Then, every hewer indented his mark on the face of the stones he had hewn and it may be of interest to visit this building and observe how carefully this was adhered to. You can by these means nearly ascertain how many hewers were employed, how the structure was built up round and round, and how those most expert in their craft had allotted to them the stones to dress which required the greatest skill.

'I have seen the same marks on buildings which I have examined all over the country. I had a hobby for collecting masons' marks some years ago and visited many of the principal cathedrals and buildings in England. I made a large collection and it is a custom I should like to see revived as, in my opinion, it would not deface the stone if done with the delicate and enduring touch which those old masons gave to work to which they attached a high value. I believe that a comparison of these marks is not only instructive but interesting to those people who, like myself, look upon masons' marks as archaeologically valuable in connection with the building history of our country.'[24]

Towards the end of the nineteenth century, the importance of geometry and the influence of the medieval mason were similarly felt by the Catalan architect Antoni Gaudí (1852-1926), who wrote: 'The Gothic forms, ciphers and devices are not fully understood by the mass of the public after four centuries of neglect.'[25]

Gowans's hope was echoed in the twentieth century by Dr James S. Richardson when he said during the 1949 Rhind Lectures: 'The study of masons' marks as illustrations of architectural history has not as yet been seriously undertaken. If there were some arrangement whereby masons' marks and mouldings could be collected for comparison, much could be done in the matter of identifying different schools or groups or even individual masons.'[26]

PART TWO : 1858 - 1863

'Passion can create drama out of inert stone.' (Le Corbusier)

Apart from interest shown by a few sympathetic admirers in Scotland, the architecture and building theories of Sir James Gowans are today still unknown—in contrast, for example, to his French contemporary Viollet-le-Duc (1814-79), whose *Dictionnaire* (1854-68) and *Entretiens* (1863 & 1872) later enjoyed the esteem of Frank Lloyd Wright and Sir Nikolaus Pevsner and whom Sir John Summerson described in 1947 as 'the last great theorist of modern architecture'.[27]

James Gowans and Viollet-le-Duc had this in common — their approach to architecture was essentially rational. It did not spring from a religious bias in favour of Gothic, a Puginesque fanaticism for the Middle Ages. On the contrary, it was based on sound knowledge of architectural principles, whether Gothic or Classic, and a practical appreciation of the potential of building materials, whether stone or iron.

In his memorable essay on Viollet-le-Duc, Sir John Summerson's description of the architect's education is equally applicable to Gowans: 'The architect's education must, therefore, proceed in two stages. First, he must learn to analyse the masterpieces of the past; then he must learn to make his own synthesis, serving the conditions and using the materials dictated by his age.'[28]

This synthesis is what Gowans achieved.

In 1858, James Gowans built a house to his own design on the south side of Edinburgh in the district of Merchiston, near Merchiston Castle, the fifteenth-century tower-house of the Napiers. His house, known appropriately as Rockville[29], was an experiment in building rationally with a traditional material.

C

Gowans stated that in designing Rockville he had had no desire to create a novelty; all he wished to do was design a building, which would test in a practical way what could be achieved by an honest use of materials, based on certain geometric principles. Gowans was eloquent on the value of geometry, as he believed 'it led not only to order and regularity but facility in combining the different parts of my design'.[30]

The most radical element of Gowans's plan was his use of a 2 ft module[31] in the form of a sandstone grid, which gave Rockville 'a curious kenspeckle look — the panels when viewed from a distance looking like so many cavities or pigeon-holes'.[32] The importance of this house cannot be over-emphasised: any textbook on nineteenth-century architecture which discusses Johnston & Walter's Jayne Building, Philadelphia (1849-50), Butterfield's All Saints' (1849-59), Paxton's Crystal Palace (1851) or Webb's Red House (1859) and omits Gowans's Rockville is incomplete. It is not being fanciful to speculate on Gowans's reactions had he been alive to examine Auguste Perret's church of Notre Dame du Raincy (1922-3). The north, south and east façades of this church consist of a grille of open panels, made up of 2 ft square precast slabs, each containing geometric apertures filled with coloured glass. Just as Rockville's grid projected beyond the surface of the rubble infill, so the church's reinforced concrete panels projected beyond the glass infill. Although Rockville's success as a structural experiment was limited by the very nature of the material, Gowans's use of a standardised grid, expressed *visibly* in all the elevations, was highly original. (The modular system was not in use in the United States until the 1890s.)

Gowans, it is clear, was attempting to plan his building by using a 2 ft module, vertically and horizontally, and deliberately emphasised the geometric rigidity and consistency of his design by a stone grid or 'frame', with some of the horizontal units used to bind the rubble infill, behind which were 2-3 ft of bonded rubble. Unlike most of his architectural contemporaries, Gowans realised that the various parts of any building could be co-ordinated by the use of a modular system. The applied 'frame' expresses his design approach, in which every detail occurs deliberately on the planning grid, not off it arbitrarily or whimsically.

Gowans was also convinced that by restricting the lines and details of his house to the semicircle and 22½, 45 and 67½ degrees, he had at last succeeded in discovering the key to medieval masonry construction. The reason why his angles are so consistent, i.e. right angles, threequarter right angles, half right angles and quarter right angles, was that such a limited choice enabled him to standardise, wherever possible, windows, doors and other details, with resultant economic benefits:

'This idea of designing upon squares and fixed angles, although new to me, must have been known to the master-masons, who produced the best examples of those styles of architecture which we so much admire. These lines are more observable in the Gothic than in other styles. From the experience I have had in drawing the details of this building, I can understand how our old master-masons were able to revel in endless design and combination of figures.'[30]

Another of his aims was to arrange the colours of his materials in such a way as to bring out the details of the building to their best advantage. The question of exactly from where Gowans obtained his stones has always aroused local speculation; the chief surmise was that Rockville incorporated stones from every quarry in Scotland, while another was that there were, in addition, stones from England and the Continent. The *Daily Scotsman,* however, was more explicit as to the precise locations from where Gowans obtained his materials:

'The two lower courses of the building are wholly composed of specimens of old rocks, such as granites, traps, etc. Above this level on the north and east fronts, with the exception of six panels above the main entrance, the rubble is principally from the brown or crop rock of Redhall mixed with fossil from the same source and quartz from Perthshire. On each side of the main entrance, which is placed to the south, the panels represent various Scottish metals, such as iron, copper and lead.

The panels immediately above are filled with specimens from the Braid Hills [near Edinburgh], while the upper storey of the west front is built chiefly with material from China, which in nature is somewhat like the porphyries of Argyleshire.'[34]

In the grounds of Rockville was laid out an acre of sunken garden, planted with rhododendrons and forsythia, wild roses and cypress trees. A garden-walk, bordered with box, led from the conservatory at the rear of the house round the wing of the coach-house to the front, where Rockville's stables looked on to a cobbled yard and across to a lodge.

The lodge was used most likely to house the gardener or some of the servants. Gowans employed the same modular grid in his window designs to form square-headed lights. Gables were chevroned rather than crow-stepped and what proved to be a delightful leitmotiv throughout his works was his use of a stone corbel in the shape of a stepped bracket, the 'treads' of which were decorated by an edge-roll moulding:

'In dressing the stones roughly and by the use of one simple geometrical form of moulding, I have endeavoured to produce a rich effect by the frequent repetition of this moulding wherever such was necessary.'[35] Much of the visual-tactile success of Gowans's buildings rests on the contrast between roughness of the masses and delicacy of the mouldings.

Apart from the lodge's curiously shaped chimneys and intricate masonry around the upper-floor gabled windows, the strongest feature was the lodge's colour. Gowans's choice of quartz, granite and sandstone as the main materials for the smaller building, and the deep reddish-ochre of its rubble infill, was brilliant in conception; the overall effect of lightness and sparkle provided an excellent contrast to the sombre richness of Rockville. The lodge, far from being the humble relation of Rockville, acted as a complement to the larger building — each set off the features, details and colours of the other. The lodge bore the mark of an architect fully conscious of his skills and appreciative of the results that could be achieved from working with stone.

Rockville, itself, square in plan and three storeys high,

was built on a site later to form the corner of Napier Road
and Spylaw Road. On the ground and first floors Gowans
standardised the width of his windows and on the top floor
arranged his windows with boldly projecting hoods. The windows
were among the details of Rockville to which Gowans attached
great importance as he considered that they enhanced the
structural effect of the skeleton of the building: 'The windows
stand out as separate designs, springing from the lower base
of the building and extending to the apex of the tympanum;
and while they form integral parts of the skeleton of the building,
they contribute to the general effect.'[36]

The design of his windows was as fascinating as the variety
of other features employed throughout the house. On Rockville's extraordinary roofline Gowans's exuberance showed itself
in massive stone chimneys, some with Gothic gables, others
with semicircular pediments, and all surmounted by castellated
chimney-pots, which caused them to resemble outsize rooks
of some grotesque chess-set. If the effect was picturesque, it
was also balanced by logic: 'With chimney-heads, you will
never have a good draught in chimneys that are thin after
passing through the level of the roof. Unless they are thick,
the current gets chilled and choked, owing to the cold damp
air it meets with from the thinness of the masonry; and further-
more, it leads to disfigurements by the use of cans, cowls and
suchlike contrivances, of what the architect should make one
of the most telling features.'[37]

The influence of Gothic architecture and of David Bryce
on Gowans was apparent in the chateau roof and balconies,
enclosed by ornate cast-iron trellises set continuously in the
shape of the initial *G*. Gowans's delight in contrasting ironwork against masonry is reminiscent in some ways later of
Gaudí's strong liking for this treatment, e.g. the Casa Figueras,
Barcelona (1900-2).

It has been suggested[38] that the tower in the south-east
corner of the building was derived from the Merchants' Steeple,
Glasgow (1665). According to Dr David Simpson, however,
Rockville's five-storey tower, adorned by a cupola, gilt ball

and spire, was an Oriental conception, prompted by the recent spell of employment in Calcutta of Moxey Sheppard, Gowans's clerk of works. It was this 64 ft tower, commanding a view as far west as Ben Lomond, which gave rise to Rockville being known inaccurately though affectionately later in Edinburgh as 'The Pagoda'.

At each level of the tower the mullions looped the loop to form deep bull's-eyes above round-headed lights. Another detail of the mullions was their decoration with examples of masons' marks collected by Gowans and carved in the stonework with great care by his masons. These marks were also to be seen on the walls of the lodge and on the coping-stones of Rockville's garden walls.

The garden was overlooked at the rear of the house by two bas-reliefs by William Brodie, RSA, of James Gowans and his elder brother Walter applied at first-floor level. Walter Gowans (a railway engineer, who later laid tracks in northern Sweden) was shown sculpting a bust; James Gowans was portrayed in the role of what he would have liked to have been in the Middle Ages — the master-mason, seen in deep study over sheets of geometric designs with a pair of compasses at his feet (only his square and mallet were missing). Among the rhododendrons in the garden stood a Classical statue of Mother With Children, one of two designed by Gowans's father-in-law, William Brodie, RSA. The other statue, now situated in West Princes Street Gardens, was formerly in the garden of Rockville as a sculpture also representing Motherhood. The play on Gowans's name which occasionally showed itself in Rockville was evident in the design by Gowans of a hall-table (later used as a garden-table), the 5 x 5 in square legs of which were delicately carved with gowans (Scots for wild daisies).

In addition to the modular grid, the most memorable and enjoyable feature of Rockville was the spectacular use of colour; Rockville was to be seen at its best in the soft northern light of an afternoon in autumn, when the vivid colours of its stonework could be subtly revealed by the lowering sun. These colours varied from salmon-pink, crimson and olive to nut-brown, blood-orange and tinges of black, all contrasted sharply by carefully positioned small chunks of glittering quartz.

The interior of the house was understated and regulated in its treatment. The entrance-hall was decorated by a series of glass windows, beautifully painted by Gowans's second wife, Mary (*née* Brodie)[39]; the Gowans crest of a lion's head langued and a motif incorporating interlocking *G*s were each encircled by the Gowans motto *Quod Ero Spero* against a background of thistles, roses and shamrocks with dazzling borders of daisies (gowans). Elsewhere, Gowans limited himself to a repetition of edge-roll mouldings and plain wooden panelling in the Perpendicular style. Other details included filigree wrought-iron gaslight fittings on the newel posts, a variety of marble fireplaces, an inviting marble bath, and a large austere kitchen with the stern motto 'Waste Not Want Not' over a large range, decorated with Dutch tiles.

Some idea of the spaciousness of Rockville can be gained from the dimensions of some of the rooms: the hall, for example, was 18 x 14 ft, the business room measured 20 x 14 ft, the dining room was 24 x 16 ft, the drawing room, also, was 24 x 16 ft and the staircase was 12 ft square. Gowans predetermined that the length, breadth and height of all his rooms were multiples of 2 ft.

In a paper read to members of the Architectural Institute of Scotland, Gowans enlarged upon the principles on which he had attempted to base his design of Rockville. He believed that the interior, not only of Rockville but of any building, should be so arranged as to suit the requirements of its occupants, and that the exterior should be designed with a view to the proper application of the building materials. Gowans discussed the first idea in depth, revealing some of the influence of Bryce and Burn:

'The principal rooms nowadays should be so situated as to command the best views of the locality and the greatest share of sunlight; at the same time, they should be so placed that they shall all have ready access from a corridor and also ready access to and from each other. In the case of the dining room, the servants' access should be distinct from that of the public. The kitchen and servants' working quarters should have a distinct and separate portion of the building allotted to them, so placed as to give the servants private and ready access to the day and night portions of the house, and ready access to the principal entrance-door, without having to pass through the corridor or saloon.

'The principal bedrooms should be of a large size and high in the ceiling, and have easy access to and from the stair-landing. The principal bedrooms in Rockville enter from a spacious lobby, lit and ventilated by a well-hole up to the roof, which also supplies light and ventilation to the attic rooms.'[40]

Hot water and gaslight were laid on to all parts of the house and one far-sighted idea was that rainwater was brought down from the roof by pipes set *inside* the walls, so as not to detract from the beauty of the façades.

Contemporary opinion was uncertain about so unorthodox a design. Of Rockville, the editor of the *Builder* could only say limply: 'We shall not annoy Mr Gowans if we do not offer any great admiration of the external appearance of the house because he, himself, does not point to it as anything than the result of a first experiment.'[41]

H. S. Goodhart-Rendel offered a more detailed critical appreciation of Rockville during the 1945-6 Sidney Jones Lectures in Art at the University of Liverpool:

'In the matter of convenience I find no fault with his plan, except on behalf of the servants generally with their sky-lighted sitting room; and of the butler in particular, who has to wash up at a sink without any draining-board in the corner of his tiny pantry, diagonally opposite to the only window, that over the door. It is, in fact, for its date, an unusually good plan, with the lines of communication very well laid down and with very well-shaped rooms . . . . The tower, according to accepted Victorian tradition, rises above the w.c., but where is its back wall, what supports its internal corner? And that noble square pavilion at the north-west angle which comes down over part only of the business room and throws the window of that room out of the middle and all crooked with the fireplace! Mr Gowans, in fact, laid the foundations for architecture very well and then built upon them not what they implied but what he thought would look nice.'[42]

This last remark might leave the reader with the false impression that in his design of Rockville, Gowans was deliberately hankering for the picturesque and the possibilities of contrived emotional effect. If so, the reason may be that, not having visited Rockville and judging it only from illustrations in the *Builder*, H. S. Goodhart-Rendel had made an assessment of Gowans based on a misunderstanding of his intentions and theories — just as he misinterpreted the complexity of a later architect, Charles Rennie Mackintosh. Clearly, he did not appear to have been aware that Rockville, far from being a Scottish Sezincote or Hafod, was a prototype, the basis of which could form the design of almost any type of building, whether it be a villa, cottage, church, museum, school, warehouse or railway station.

The achievement of James Gowans reveals itself in his attempt by the middle of the nineteenth century to create modular architecture which was economically realistic and visually satisfying and imaginative.

This fusion of romanticism and rationalism (i.e. maximum variety and maximum standardisation) is as evident in Gowans's Rockville as it is in Peter Ellis's Oriel Chambers, Liverpool (1864); Mackintosh's Scotland Street School, Glasgow (1904); Perret's church of Notre Dame du Raincy, near Paris (1922-3); or Peter Womersley's Nuffield Transplantation Surgery Unit, Western General Hospital, Edinburgh (1964-8)[43]. However diverse in style and materials these buildings are, they have three qualities, at least, in common — articulate expression of structure, design unity and visual impact. A building may be adequate, technically and functionally, but unless it evokes from the layman a critical response, a sense of involvement, then, as a work of architectural art, it is a failure — a dead 'thing' rather than a living force.

The value of creative enjoyment, which is reflected in Gowans's work, has been enlarged upon — admittedly in a different context — by Gordon Cullen: 'A wholly satisfying and virile architecture cannot flourish unless, in its practice, social justification is lavishly compounded with personal pleasure, a wholesome delight in the creative process as well as an appreciation of the end in view. There is no need to regard such naïve delight as almost sinful, since without the ingredient of sensuous enjoyment the practice of architecture must inevitably degenerate into little more than a sordid routine, or at the most the execution of mere intellectual cleverness.'[44]

That Rockville was seen by Gowans not as an isolated *tour de force* but, on the contrary, as a prototype is apparent in the closely related designs of Lammerburn (10 Napier Road) and 23 & 25 Blacket Place in Edinburgh; Lochee Station in Dundee; a cottage and farm buildings at Gowanbank in West Lothian; and two cottages at Redhall, near his earlier group of 1857.

The following year, in 1859, Gowans designed another large and intricate house called Lammerburn[45], which still stands at the present day on the opposite corner site of Napier Road and Spylaw Road. By designing it in close harmony with the structural appearance of Rockville and using the same materials, Gowans imparted a sense of unity to this future pocket of suburban Edinburgh and succeeded in balancing the dramatic splendour of Rockville.

Lammerburn, two storeys in height, is the third major example of James Gowans's highly idiosyncratic vocabulary, incorporating his beliefs in geometry as a fundamental principle of architectural design and the value of a grid in facilitating standardisation and co-ordination of design elements. What is particularly noticeable about Gowans's handling of Lammerburn is his desire for precision, colour and bold proportions. Whether it be in his design of a coom ceiling or banisters or the care lavished on a single chimney or window, one is always conscious of Gowans's complete sympathy with the materials he was working with and of his complete control over the stages leading to the final creation. The slender narrow lights of the windows are set at angles, protected by projecting gables, each of which is supported by the ubiquitous stone brackets, which are among his personal trademarks.

Gowans's checked passion breaks out in his designs of Lammerburn's sturdy chimneys, which seem to rise up like pillars through the steeply pitching, slate-covered roof. Lammerburn's complex, picturesque silhouette and robust detailing would have appealed as much to the Greenes as to the Grimms. People remember this house long after it has lodged its image in their minds, just as a picnic can be recalled by grains of sand found in a jacket pocket weeks after the summer holidays.

An interesting quality of Lammerburn is its curiously wooden appearance, doubtless owing to its lattice grid and crusty, tactile masonry, with its shades of brown, burnt sienna, rust and coloured quartz. Throughout Lammerburn and all Gowans's other buildings of that period there is an analogy with English Tudor timber-framing, Tyrolean chalets, traditional rural log-houses in central and northern Europe and, in particular, with the Stick Style of architecture, i.e. the wood-sawn components which decorated so successfully the exteriors of many eastern American houses (c. 1840-76), and the later Shingle Style. This similarity is borne out most strongly by Gowans's use of wooden brackets — admittedly less intricate than their American equivalents — which support the deeply overhanging eaves of Lammerburn and Redhall Bank Cottages.

Although medieval masons, on occasions, were not averse to imitating masonry forms by the use of timber construction, Gowans's use of wooden brackets as an alternative to stone is as interesting as his choice of stone-carved shingles on the sides of window-gables as a substitute for ordinary slates. The play of intervals and shadows between these brackets, with their change of levels and spatial rhythms, cause them to resemble thin sculptures which vary in effect and appearance when seen from different angles and in changing light.

In that same year, 1859, Gowans contributed to the RSA

Exhibition in Edinburgh a design for a row of railway workers' houses in Crieff.

In 1860-1, James Gowans and his wife moved to Merchiston to live in Rockville for the next twenty-five years until 1886. It was a period which was to prove exciting and lucrative for Gowans in a variety of ways.

At Westminster, for example, Disraeli and Gladstone were soon to turn political life into a highly gladiatorial contest, followed eagerly by the Victorian public and the press. Although it might seem that Gowans was a Radical or pioneer Socialist, with his concern for the working class, this was not the case. Even though at one stage he was vice-president of the Advanced Liberal Association in Edinburgh, Gowans soon joined the wing of the Conservative Party which was increasingly critical of ruthless employers, bad working conditions for employees and the doctrine of *laissez-faire*. Just as some of Philip Webb's clients were enlightened Conservatives, interested in industrial and social problems, so many landowners felt a growing responsibility towards their employees. Nowadays, it tends to be forgotten that Conservative Working-Men's Associations and Clubs flourished in the latter half of the nineteenth century.

During this period, much of Gowans's time was devoted to architecture, railway engineering, the management of his quarries and visiting his racehorses stabled in Yorkshire. By the second half of the nineteenth century, Gowans had established himself as the largest single lessee of quarries in Scotland. It has been recorded that in 1867, for example, Gowans was contracted to deliver a consignment of sandstone from Plean Quarry in Stirlingshire to be used in the construction of a warehouse in Paternoster Row, London, for the publishing firm of Thomas Nelson.[46]

After the City of Edinburgh's debt by 1833 had been estimated at £402,000[47] there was a pause in the 1830s and '40s. The second half of the century, however, saw great expansion; on the open lands and estates of Grange, Greenhill, Merchiston and Newington were built many plain-fronted, stone villas each with its coach-house, turreted Baronial mansions and large houses in the Italian style with campaniles.

The Blacket Estate, on the south side near Newington, planned by James Gillespie Graham (1777-1855) during the late 1820s, was the property of the British Linen Company Bank. As it was private property, the estate was guarded by lodges and gates, which were closed at dusk in order that the houses might have 'all the privacy and convenience of country residences'. The lodges and Gothic gate-piers still remain at the present day.

This development was continued in the early 1860s with two houses designed by James Gowans. These buildings still stand today between Greek villas and late nineteenth-century mansions as 23 & 25 Blacket Place. The two houses are built in a single block and comprise three storeys and a basement. Gowans's 2 ft module is again in force, binding together ashlar facings and his usual mosaic of rough, polychromatic masonry. Decorative iron railings surround the roof and adorn the bracketed window-sills. The windows all have Gowans's individual stamp of attentive care and eye for detail — semicircular pediments are prominent, keystones are carved with small, geometric patterns and daisies (gowans), and mullions are typically given projecting square set-offs, emphasising the grid's controlling lines. The grid and mosaic of polychrome rubble and quartz are very noticeable in the crow-step gables and large rectangular chimneys.

On completion, 23 Blacket Place was owned by James Somerville, SSC, whose link with the building is marked by a large painted window at the foot of the stairs; beneath the letters J S and the date, 1861, are painted the arms of the Somervilles (blue, three mullets between seven cross crosslets fitché, gold), which bear for a crest a wyvern perched upon a spear and wheel, and the family motto 'Fear God in Life'.[48]

The rational criterion to be found in Gowans's architecture is evident in Blacket Place as it is in Napier Road; in each building, his choice of module facilitated his 'bringing out all the doors, windows and finishings of one uniform size, and so admitting of their execution by machinery at a considerable reduction of costs'.[49]

During the second half of the nineteenth century, the development of Churchhill, Grange, Morningside and Newington formed part of the Victorian contribution to the changing appearance of Edinburgh. In terms of mid Victorian town planning, this development cannot be compared with a magnificent scheme like Charles Wilson's Park area in Glasgow. Yet, these suburbs are as much an integral part of Edinburgh — 'that most beautiful of all the capitals of Europe'[50] — as the multi-storey tenements of the High Street or the impressive streets, crescents and squares which form the unrivalled cultural achievement of the New Town. Dick Place, like Ann Street, admirably reflects the spirit of the period in which each was built. At a time when stone was relatively inexpensive and masons were plentiful, the houses of Edinburgh's Victorian and Edwardian suburbs are very well constructed, with large rooms, big windows and generous gardens for children to play in. Floors are often of Canadian redwood or Scandinavian pitch-pine; ceilings are decorated by richly embellished friezes (e.g. Hippolyte Blanc's drawing-room ceiling at 17 Strathearn Place); external ornamentation is usually confined to foliated consoles, decorative bargeboards and ironwork.

As in the case of most other cities, many of these nineteenth-century buildings are so large that they can no longer be maintained as family houses, with the result that many have since been converted into schools, hotels, offices, university hostels and nursing homes — if not subdivided into expensive flats or simply, of course, expediently demolished to make way for unimaginative 'junior executive' villas.

During the short span of the next three years, Gowans continued to design buildings based on his simple, economical combination of a standardised lattice grid and infill of tactile, polychromatic rockery. Minor examples of his architecture can still be seen in two delightful, square-plan cottages near his earlier pair at Redhall; one of these cottages, now 4 Redhall Bank Road, was built (c. 1863) to house the family of his quarry clerk; the other stands in the grounds of Redhall Nursery, off Lanark Road.

Two larger buildings, however, merit more attention. The first of these is a suburban railway station which, being designed by Gowans, is unique in the history of British railway architecture — Lochee Station (1861) in Dundee.

The Dundee and Newtyle Railway was incorporated in 1826 and opened in 1831. At that time, traversing the Sidlaw Hills presented a difficult problem to railway engineers; so much so, that Charles Landale's final scheme involved the construction of eleven miles of track with three steep inclines at Law (1 in 10), Balbeuchly (1 in 25) and Hatton (1 in 13) with two level stretches in between. During the decade 1849-59, after the gauge conversion from 4 ft 6½ in to 4 ft 8½ in, the line continued to be worked with cable-operated inclines; in short, for almost thirty years, the success of the railway had been seriously handicapped by the three steep gradients. In 1859, the Dundee and Newtyle Railways Improvement Act authorised two major deviations — from Rose Mill to Auchterhouse and from south of Baldovan to Ninewells Junction.

In June 1861, Dundee and Newtyle Railway traffic was diverted from Dundee West via the Lochee Deviation, which thus enabled the Law incline and Dundee (Ward Road) Station to be closed. New stations were built, the most beautiful of which was at Lochee.

As a result of this realignment carried out by Gowans in the early 1860s, the Dundee and Newtyle Railway operated from Dundee West as far as Ninewells Junction, where it branched off round the west side of the Law and then turned eastwards through Liff and Lochee; curving north after Lochee, Fairmuir Junction was reached, from where the lines ran north through Baldovan, Baldragon, Rose Mill, Dronley, Pitnappie to Newtyle — a distance of sixteen miles.

Although Lochee Station was similar in general outline to Newtyle Station (1830-1), railway passengers must have expressed considerable surprise and delight at first seeing Gowans's

station — even Ruskin might have made an exception of
Lochee Station.

Throughout the entire horizontal shape of the building,
Gowans's 2 ft module is rigidly applied, with the grid binding
together a richly tactile mosaic of coral-pink, paprika-red, rust
and black rubble, highlighted by a speckling of random chunks
of glittering quartz. The effect once more lends itself to a comparison with timber framing; of particular interest, perhaps,
is Gowans's intelligent use of identical, timber moulded brackets
for the wooden platform roof and stone moulded brackets for
the rest of the building — the eye sees only continuity and
uniformity.

As an example of nineteenth-century railway architecture,
Lochee Station displays on a miniature scale the same geometric
simplicity, imaginativeness of design and architectural understanding of materials as King's Cross Station, London, planned
by Lewis Cubitt (1799-1883) in 1850 and built in the following
two years.

For several years, Lochee Station was closed to passengers
— its platform derelict and litter-strewn, its flower-beds uprooted
and the glass panes of its ornate iron lamps cracked. A policy
of enlightenment prevailed in Dundee, however, and in the
autumn of 1972 the property was bought for preservation and
a new function by Lochee Burns Club.

Shortly after the completion of Lochee Station, Gowans
gave his attention to Gowanbank in West Lothian, where his
father had died of phthisis on 7 April 1858 aged sixty-nine.
James Gowans had earlier (c. 1857) altered the original building
by removing the eaves to make it bell-cast. Rhododendrons
and thickly clustered conifers give the approachway to the house
a sombre, melancholy atmosphere. Cornices are bracketed, tall
chimneys are incised with vertical ribs and decorated with
tooth-edged chimney-heads. Gowans turned the house into a
small country mansion, to which he could retreat from the
atmosphere of business offices and dusty quarries and spend
the summer months with his family.

On a section of land lower down from the house, Gowans built a group of farm-sheds in local rubble and with standardised stone slabs. These polychromatic buildings display a variety of rough-textured and picturesque chimneys, complete with lattice grid, moulded brackets and castellated chimney-tops; the flues are either square or circular, with the standardised vertical units being 'bound' by the horizontals, like a tied-up bunch of sticks. Beneath the set-off across a window (later bricked-up) Gowans inscribed the following:

Heb. III 4

For Every House Is Builded By Some Man
But He That Build All Things is God

Eccles. II 4 XI XII

1 August 1862

Among the grouping of byres and storage-sheds, Gowans also designed a cottage for a farm labourer's family in a style similar to Redhall Bank Cottages and Rockville's lodge. The two-storey cottage, with its boldly shaped windows, chimneys and gables, is still occupied; it displays compactness, intricacy of detail and a *building* craftsmanship, often lacking in many similar buildings of the same period by other architects.

The deep earthen colours of tobacco and walnut-brown are sharply contrasted by Gowans's random disposition of quartz. The cottage's large chimney-breast incorporates the grid and mosaic of rubble masonry, the colours and pattern of which are found nowadays no longer (or rarely) in architecture but in abstract paintings: the entire surface is a riot of rose-petal pink, pigeon-grey, purple, brown and ochre — closer chromatically, perhaps, to the rough, earth-coloured stones of Gaudí's Casa Figueras and lodges in the Parque Güell, Barcelona, than to such crudely coloured buildings as Elvetham Hall, Hampshire (Teulon) or Keble College Chapel, Oxford (Butterfield).

Here there is an obligation to make a brief digression and enlarge upon this comparison. To convey Gowans's colour-sense by analogy with a Mediterranean architect's should not surprise

D

anyone equally familiar with the works of the highly gifted Scottish watercolourist, Arthur Melville (1855-1904). In paintings such as *Autumn — Loch Lomond* or *A Mediterranean Port,* both in Glasgow Art Gallery, Melville expresses boldly the Scots' keen eye for colour. It is this Scottish-Continental sympathy and common exultation in colour which helps to explain why the Scottish Border textile industry has attracted such a radical ally and practitioner in Bernat Klein; why Mackintosh's chairs and interior designs have gained such an enthusiastic critic in Filippo Alison; and why J. D. Fergusson's paintings have been praised for their 'outspoken, ringing colours' by André Dunoyer de Segonzac. It is this rapport which simultaneously shows up the introspection and aesthetic indifference of the English, a nation whose artistic temperament is best expressed not in the plastic or visual arts but in literature, particularly poetry.

One architectural journalist's observation that throughout Rockville (and the buildings which followed) 'joints in the grid were everywhere expressed with little square projections as though a close-knit concrete frame were poking through'[51] (see p. 29), is equally applicable to the cottage at Gowanbank. In the corner recess above each window, Gowans humorously 'signed' his building by an arrangement of stones in the shape of gowans.

What contributes to the visual enjoyment of Gowans's architecture is the way in which these farm buildings are designed and constructed in complete harmony with the surrounding landscape and in natural colours which blend at a distance with the soil, trees and walls.

Gowanbank is now in the control of the National Coal Board and the property is already showing the outward signs of impersonal ownership. With the possible danger to these buildings of excessive damp and internal decay, their future gives cause for anxiety. They should be preserved along with all Gowans's remaining buildings to arouse curiosity in future generations and as Gowans's contribution to Victorian rural architecture.

Seen in perspective against the main stream of mid Victorian architecture, James Gowans's buildings of the late 1850s and early 1860s are the products of a designer who possessed passion *and* logic, and who accepted the discipline imposed by standardisation. Gowans's individual and romantic-rational style of construction is an excellent example of the departure by some architects from the conventional, eclectic vocabularies, either of Greek or Gothic Revivalism (and, more especially, Scottish Baronial).

This claim for Gowans does necessitate, at the same time however, a brief reference to another outstanding Scottish architect who was a contemporary of Gowans — Alexander Thomson (1817-75) of Glasgow. Although this architect confined himself mainly to the Greek, Egyptian, and even Hindu, styles of architecture, he was more than a mere revivalist like Sir Robert Smirke or William Wilkins. Indeed, by his daring experiments and inventiveness, he proved to his colleagues elsewhere in Britain that even in the 1860s and early 1870s, the Greek idiom could be exploited dynamically to form the basis for a perfectly feasible, contemporary style. Many of Thomson's ideas were as subtle, far-sighted and original as those of Gowans, e.g. Thomson's use of glass dome lights, clear varnish and continuous glazing, set directly into iron mullions entirely separate from load-bearing colonnades.

James Gowans's buildings can be described as a decisive repudiation of arbitrariness and irrationalism, an affirmation of the importance of proportion, rhythm and scale; in consequence, the modular stone grid of his design vocabulary has more in common with the standardised, repetitive components of the twentieth century than with the lavishly ornamented historico-religious façades of his own period.

PART THREE : 1864 - 1890

*'Style is a unity of principle animating all the work of an epoch,
the result of a state of mind which has its own special character.'*
(Le Corbusier)

By the 1860s and 1870s, a deep reaction had set in amongst
many architects against the insipid and pedantic Gothick style,
practised by their predecessors. They objected strongly to this
debasement of architecture because, in the main, it was the
outcome of an essentially literary-antiquarian age, given to
the veneration of medievalism in the form of poems and novels.
Buildings such as Strawberry Hill, Belvoir Castle or Abbotsford
were highly picturesque but as examples of contemporary architecture they were artificial and historicist, built deliberately to
reflect the whims of their owners.

What Butterfield, Lamb, Teulon, Waterhouse and their
colleagues sought after was to continue building Gothic architecture, drawing heavily on Anglo-French and Italian sources,
but by using materials such as coloured brick, granite, iron,
marble and terracotta to establish Victorian Gothic as the
'modern style'. This, they hoped, would help to solve the problem
of a distinct and easily recognisable architectural style of the
nineteenth century.

At the start of Part Two, it was mentioned that Gowans
and Viollet-le-Duc had in common a rational approach to
architecture, which rejected the idea of revivalism. In his essay
on Viollet-le-Duc, Sir John Summerson has written lucidly of
the basic difference between the French theorist and his English
contemporaries, men like Pugin, Butterfield, Scott, Street and
Pearson: 'All of them were as deeply imbued with a love of
Gothic architecture as was Viollet-le-Duc, but not one of them
was man enough to *think his way through* the romantic attraction

of style to a philosophic point of view applicable to all buildings at all times.'[52]

Consequently, the High Victorian style became synonymous with an exuberant, highly eclectic integration of Gothic and Renaissance motifs, uniting vividly coloured materials and rich, naturalistic ornamentation. If this confusion led, as it did in many instances, to sheer coarseness and vagueness of expression, it was also responsible for renewing an interest in and concern for skilled craftsmanship with stone, iron, glass, brick and glazed tile. Prominent in this revival were William Morris, Edward Burne-Jones, John Powell, De Morgan, the O'Sheas and, of course, William Burges — an architect who, with the designs of Cardiff Castle and his own house in Melbury Road, London, created some of the most colourful and exotic interiors of High Victorian Gothic buildings.

Experiments with hard, shiny materials and bold, sculptural shapes were developed even farther by those architects of the nineteenth century who were labelled by H. S. Goodhart-Rendel as 'rogues', i.e. architects who were driven or who chose to practise apart from the herd. They included, among others, Edward Lamb, Thomas Harris, R. L. Roumieu, Bassett Keeling, Edward Prior and F. T. Pilkington. The last named is worthy of mention in any account of Victorian architecture in general and of Gowans's work in particular.

Frederick Thomas Pilkington (1832-98), who has been aptly described by David Walker as 'the great *fauve* of Scottish Victorian architecture'[53], will be remembered primarily as a church architect, displaying great boldness of and care for shapes and details. His inspiration from Ruskin's eulogy of Venetian Gothic, a liking for vigorous, sculptural shapes and a curious, accidental foretaste of Catalan Renaixença architecture[54] can be found in such buildings as Trinity Church, Irvine (1861); the Barclay Church, Edinburgh (1863); Penicuik South Church (1863); St. John's, Kelso (1865); St. Mark's, Dundee (1868). Pilkington was also responsible for a number of houses, some of the finest of which are in Edinburgh and Penicuik.

Just as Gowans had a preference for polychromatic masonry,

moulded brackets, castellated chimneys and cast-ironwork, so
Pilkington had a liking for angular, warlike chimneys, carved
vegetable decoration and pilastered window-frames (usually of
sandstone or granite).

In a short appreciation of Scottish Victorian architecture,
Colin McWilliam has commented: 'And there are the buildings,
also, whose extraordinary originality defies the attempt to place
them in any stylistic pigeon-hole. Such are the works of F. T.
Pilkington . . . and of Sir James Gowans.'[55]

Nine years before his collaboration with Pilkington, James
Gowans was involved as architect of the tenement development
at the south end of Castle Terrace in Edinburgh. This spectacular scheme, designed in 1866, of some dozen tenements
in a continuous block, four and five storeys high with basements,
was Gowans's attempt at tempering the spirit behind High
Victorian Gothic with his own beliefs in the value of geometric
proportions, well-finished construction and standardisation of
details. Although the grid of squares was not made visible on this
occasion, the designs were still based on multiples of 2 ft and
angles of 22½, 45 and 67½ degrees. With its profusion of edge-roll
mouldings, standardised brackets, semicircular pediments, bull's-
eye windows and terrifyingly steep roofline, encrusted with gables,
shingles, ironwork and battery of castellated chimneys, Castle
Terrace is the finest example in Edinburgh of the complexity
and self-assurance of the High Victorian Gothic style.

In 1868, the *Builder* wrote of Gowans's scheme: 'The
first instalment of the new buildings in Castle Terrace by James
Gowans, in his own peculiar style, is now completed. The
peculiarity consists in the ignoring of every known detail, and
the application of mouldings more suited for execution in wood
than in stone. The general effect produced by the number of
gables, moulded chimneys and statues breaking the skyline is
striking and picturesque.'[56]

Although 25-36 Castle Terrace was planned by Gowans as
a whole block of street architecture, No. 27 is distinguished
by two five-storey columns of projecting three-sided windows,

each of which is 'crowned' at the top by slate-covered cupolas. Number 29, too, has an imaginative silhouette; the corner elevation of this building, now the Queen's Institute of District Nursing (formerly Queen Victoria's Jubilee Institute for Nurses), is emphasised by the focal-point of a statue of the youthful Victoria, gazing down on two cherub-like attendant figures on either side of a large, gabled window. Gowans's interest in the history of the medieval mason showed itself by a mottling of masons' marks over the surface of gables and upper walls.

In 1869, the *Builder* continued its description of Gowans's architecture, completed a year later with four adjoining blocks of flats at 11, 13, 15 & 17 Cornwall Street: 'In this neighbourhood of the West End, James Gowans is proceeding with the second block of houses in Castle Terrace; those already erected have an effective skyline broken by high-pitched gables and ornamented chimney-shafts, but we cannot reconcile ourselves to the so-called geometric details — its novelty is its only merit. In the interior arrangements, Mr Gowans has also departed from the usual routine and here we meet with things more worthy of approval. For example, dark bedrooms in the centre of a corner block are entirely got rid of — "a consummation devoutly to be wished". The water-closets are all ventilated from the outside and [like Rockville] a ventilating-pipe is carried from the drains up the chimney-shafts to prevent the possibility of foul air entering the houses.'[57]

Gowans's plan was completed by his own purchase of part of the grounds opposite Castle Terrace for a boulevard, which he decided to leave open for the benefit of the general public; the remainder he intended to rail off and lay out as private gardens for the local flat-owners.

In a lecture given to members of the Edinburgh Architectural Association in 1870, a certain W. G. Shiells declared: 'Would that we had more citizens like James Gowans. Look at the spirit he has displayed in the laying-out of Castle Terrace. You may object to the style of building, but peculiar as they are in detail, they are picturesque in outline and far more pleasing to look at than the stale inanity of their neighbours.'[58]

Gowans had no sooner completed this scheme than he found himself engaged on a project of a very different nature.

Before 1871, travelling in and beyond Edinburgh was mainly by horse-drawn carriage — longer journeys required the train. By the 1870s, though, the increase in population and the expansion of the city's boundaries necessitated some form of improvement in urban transport.

In 1871, the Edinburgh Street Tramways Company was formed as a result of the Edinburgh Tramways Act. With a capital investment of £300,000 the company was given the task of planning a system of tramways in Edinburgh and Leith. The company's engineer was John Macrae and the contract for laying the lines was awarded to James Gowans — partly because of his past railway experience.

In *Edinburgh's Transport* (1964), D. L. G. Hunter mentions Gowans and has explained how he used a system of wrought-iron rails with a gauge of 4 ft 8½ in on horizontal timbers embedded in concrete. (All British, West European and United States railways are of 4 ft 8½ in narrow gauge.) In November 1871, work had progressed so rapidly that the first section of tramway was opened to the public between Haymarket and the Bridges. Ten tramcars of German manufacture were each drawn along the track by a pair of horses.[59]

In the mid 1870s, Gowans resumed practice in architecture in his new office at 31 Castle Terrace and, with a small group of businessmen, promoted a plan to build a new theatre, winter garden and aquarium as 'part of a great scheme for public recreation and amusement' between Cornwall Street and Cambridge Street off Castle Terrace.

The New Edinburgh Theatre was designed by James Gowans in collaboration with F. T. Pilkington and his partner J. Murray Bell (1839-77). Gowans was responsible for the design of the exterior with the original intention of relating the theatre to his earlier buildings nearby; the monumental façade, massive in scale, extended 300 ft along Castle Terrace and was entered by a 30 ft high central doorway.

The building was to have been flanked by four crown-capped towers (octagonal in shape, like 27 Castle Terrace), the inner pair rising to 100 ft and the outer to 150 ft. As a result of insufficient capital, however, Gowans was forced to modify his plans[60] — the four towers were abandoned in favour of a large, square dome, and the roof was surmounted by a parapet on which stood large urns as substitutes for more expensive statues of the Muses. The wings were designed (but not built) to accommodate a winter garden, an aquarium and a concert room.

Pilkington and Bell, who were responsible for the theatre's interior, were reputed to have visited every major theatre and opera-house in England and on the Continent in order to assimilate the finest features of each in their final designs. The auditorium was 5,000 sq ft; the pit and stalls held 1,000 seats; the dress circle and boxes, 400; the second circle, 600; the gallery, 1,000, allowing for 3,000 altogether. The proscenium was 32 ft wide x 32 ft high with a width behind of 74 ft, expanding backwards to 114 ft. The stage was designed to make use of the latest equipment, including hydraulic machinery for scene-shifting. Gowans insisted on spaciousness in the foyer, staircases and public rooms and succeeded in providing ample ventilation and a comfortable temperature, controlled by steam-pipes in winter and a large punkah in summer. Pilkington's choice of interior decoration was influenced by the contemporary French taste for white, blue and gold with a painted ceiling representing the open sky, flecked with fleecy clouds.

In December 1875, the New Edinburgh Theatre was officially opened at a cost of £80,000 and caused the *Builder* to proclaim: 'It may be safely pronounced to be one of the most elegant and complete theatres in the kingdom.'[61] Unfortunately, the enterprise soon proved for Gowans and his associates to be a disastrous speculation. As a result of poor management, the company found itself bankrupt in 1877 and the New Edinburgh Theatre thus lasted only two years before being bought by the Synod of the United Presbyterian Church for £26,700. After alterations by the Glasgow architect John Burnet (1814-1901), the building was renamed the Synod Hall[62].

D. A. Small wrote in 1928: 'At that time there was nothing like it in Britain, either in size or grandeur, but unfortunately the time was not yet ripe for an undertaking of this magnitude, and the theatre did not receive sufficient support to make it pay.'[63] The Royal Lyceum Theatre was not opened until 1883, the King's Theatre in 1906 and the Usher Hall in 1914.

Gowans did not become wholly discouraged by this failure, for he was involved with many other social ventures. From 1868, Gowans had been a member of Edinburgh Town Council and chairman of the Public Health Committee — a position in which he was closely associated with the welfare of the working class and the improvement of the city's sanitation system.

In 1870, at the RSA Exhibition, Gowans had displayed 'Suggested Improvement of the North Bridge' (26 in x 52 in pen-and-ink drawing with a colour wash of a new North Bridge with geometric patterns and cast-iron moulded brackets); in 1873, a watercolour of workmen's houses at Drumbowie in West Lothian; and in 1874, unexecuted (?) plans of a 'Teacher's House and School for a Country Parish'. As a result of the 1872 Education (Scotland) Act, Gowans was a member of the Edinburgh School Board and chairman of the building committee for planning the first Board schools — by May 1875, sixteen schools had been built 'sanitarily, with plenty of light and air'[64].

In 1860, Gowans had advocated to members of the Architectural Institute of Scotland the establishment of a Chair of Architecture in universities with examinations and diplomas. Twenty years later, in 1880, at a meeting in Edinburgh of the National Association for the Promotion of Social Science, Gowans returned to this important topic — later, by 1891, to be an issue arousing considerable controversy:

'In addition to the powers already given to the local authority, there ought to be established, in my opinion, in our University a Chair of Architecture. By this arrangement, the position of an architect would be defined, which is not now the case.

'In the learned professions this status is maintained, and

is of great value to the community. The legal profession [in Scotland] are represented by the Faculty of Advocates, the Society of Writers to the Signet, and Solicitors before the Supreme Court; our medical men and others have their professional position defined, because they have had a systematic training through a course of years and require to pass a proper examination. It is not so with those who, in these days, write themselves down as "Architect".

'A young man, with a limited experience and probably an imperfect education, is employed in a surveyor's office for a few years, and through the influence of friends he starts business on his own account and begins to draw plans, because he makes terms with clients to do so at reduced fees. The natural result is that, in many cases, the edifice proceeds, the sanitary arrangements being entirely neglected, and water-closets and baths, which ought to be *ventilated* and well *lighted* direct from the outside, are placed in the centre and darkest part of the structure, thereby necessitating the drainage passing under the building, which is one of the most dangerous and objectionable situations for a drain to be placed in.

'We strongly urge that no man should be allowed to be employed as an architect, unless he has received his diploma under the same sanction as an ordinary medical practitioner, or has passed his examinations as creditably and responsibly as a lawyer.

'Happily, many architects can and do lead the public mind on sanitary subjects, and will not be diverted from a moral and intelligent purpose for the object of saving a little money to a speculator, who may have neither intelligence nor moral purpose. At the same time, it cannot be concealed that in the plans and drawings of houses much less care is given to the detail of what affects health than to the detail of purely secondary considerations, such as decoration and the like. The drawings of a building, which should all be registered and officially preserved, ought to show in detail the precise position of all pipes, if they cannot be seen, and the line and level of drains, as well as the position and connection of cisterns, for domestic and sanitary use.'[65]

In 1884, Gowans designed 1-4 Lockharton Gardens and 64-82 Colinton Road, nearby, overlooking the Union Canal.

The following year, in 1885, Gowans succeeded Robert Hutchison as Lord Dean of Guild — a historic Corporation office in which Gowans displayed great firmness in maintaining the exacting standards of Edinburgh's building regulations and his growing concern for public health. During his term of office, Gowans wrote a short book suitably entitled *The Maintenance of the Health of the People and the Beauty of our City* (1885).

Gowans took for his motto, 'Light and Air', and insisted that in all modern buildings ample space, light and ventilation should be the basis of planning and not the architect's obsession with the finer points of impressive façades. In this publication, Gowans gave his qualified advice on the upkeep of houses — declaring, for example, that the rear of any building should look just as attractive as the front and should not be ruined by a rash of external drainpipes. Gowans anticipated the plea put forward almost ten years later by Hermann Muthesius (1861-1927), during his famous lectures in 1896-9, for wide horizontal windows allowing 'floods of light'. Gowans stated in 1885:

'In a southern and open aspect there should be not less than one square foot of glass to every one hundred cubic feet of room space. The fashion in the architecture of the present day is to have small windows. That is, I think, to be deplored especially in cities in our northern clime, where we have so little sunlight; not only in the houses of our working people, but also in our more important buildings, such as public offices and others, there should be a flood of light.'[66]

Gowans was a strong advocate for baths at work-sites for coalminers and paraffin-workers: 'I care not whether sanitary reform is brought about by Liberal or Conservative, Gladstone or Salisbury, but it appears to me that the disestablishment of dirt, darkness and disease is an infinitely more urgent public question than that of the Church of Scotland!'[67] Gowans was convinced that what was required urgently was not only an efficient local authority health system but the appointment of a

Minister of Health, whose function would be to administer public health regulations aided by qualified local officials. His proposal was sufficiently radical for well over twenty-five years to pass before the Ministry of Health was established by the 1919 Ministry of Health Act.

As might have been expected, Gowans attacked vigorously the use of brick and cement creeping into the city's architecture and the use of paint on good stone. He pointed out the harm caused by the pollution of the Water of Leith from local distilleries, glue-works and paper-mills and suggested that the river might be conserved if all the mill-lades were abolished and the mills driven in future by steam-power instead of water-power. Gowans referred to the opportunities of making the roads and railways into the city more attractive by the planting of trees.

Gowans had a deep affection for Edinburgh and a great concern for its future architectural development: 'In conclusion, allow me to say that I trust that our architects will do honour to their profession by designing all structures, particularly ordinary dwelling-houses, so as to give stability and complete immunity from any risk to health. In laying out feuing schemes, they must give free, open and well-arranged streets and an occasional garden plot or square; they must also give us archi-tecture so that our admiration and delight shall be spontaneously elicited. Above all, I would ask them not to pander to the cravings of clients, who value money more than buildings.'[68]

In spite of Gowans's attachment to masonry construction, the important contribution of the second half of the nineteenth century to architectural development lay in the increasing use by engineers and some architects of cast-iron and glass (and since the 1880s of reinforced concrete and steel) in construction. This development was given an added impetus by the century's great phenomena — large stations, hotels, museums, bridges, warehouses and international exhibitions. Exhibitions were designed solely to provide as much space and light as possible and to be erected and dismantled in the shortest possible time.

Thus there was latent a new element in architecture — impermanence.

After the 1851 International Exhibition in London, there followed a number of similar exhibitions, notably in Paris in 1855, 1867, 1878, 1889 and 1900; in Vienna in 1873; in Philadelphia in 1876; in Glasgow in 1888 and 1901; and in Chicago in 1893.

In Scotland, a year before Queen Victoria's jubilee, an event occurred which was to mark the climax of James Gowans's entire career. In 1886, the International Exhibition of Industry, Science and Art was staged in Edinburgh, the exhibition executive committee's chairman of which was James Gowans, at sixty-five a figure of considerable popularity in Edinburgh.

This exhibition, of course, was not the first of its kind to be held in Edinburgh; in 1882, an International Fishery Exhibition had been mounted in the Waverley Market and in 1884, an International Forestry Exhibition had been held in the grounds of Donaldson's Hospital. An unsuccessful plan had even been made in 1859 for an exhibition similar in scale to the Crystal Palace to be staged in part of the Botanic Gardens in a building to have been designed by David Rhind.

The 1886 Exhibition was held in the ideal setting of the Meadows, a large expanse of flat land, drained at the start of the nineteenth century for the benefit of the public. The exhibition hall — 1,000 ft long and 300 ft wide — was designed by Sir J. J. Burnet (1857-1938) of Glasgow and consisted of two parts: a grand pavilion at the west end of the Meadows united to a 970 ft long range of courts on either side of a central corridor.

In the design of the grand pavilion, the façade of which was similar in appearance to the Palais de l'Industrie (1878) in Paris[69], the outer walls were of brick, the inner of wood and the span-roof and corner domes of iron and glass, supported on steel beams carried by cast-iron columns in concrete foundations. The building occupied seven acres.

The 1886 International Exhibition was formally opened by Prince Albert Victor on 6 May and remained open for six months. The material progress of the age was displayed in thirty-four courts, ranging from furniture, engraving, painting, jewellery and pottery to sea industries, industrial machinery, the Clyde's supremacy in world shipbuilding, locomotives, bicycles, tramcars and carriages.

The popular features of the exhibition were an Old Edinburgh display, imaginatively designed by Sydney Mitchell (1856-1930)[70], and five art galleries in which could be seen numerous works by English and Continental painters: Hogarth, Constable, Etty, Whistler, Stott of Oldham, Millet, Corot, Delacroix, Courbet and Monticelli. In addition to works by such well-known Scottish painters as Wilkie, Raeburn, Mc-Culloch, MacNee and Bough were contemporary canvases by Arthur Melville, John Lavery, T. Millie Dow and James Pryde. (Melville was elected ARSA in 1886.) Prominence was also given to Scottish photographers such as A. A. Inglis and E. R. Yerbury and to sculptors such as J. S. Rhind and D. W. Stevenson.

Foreign exhibits were entered from all over the world: French perfumes and inks, Turkish embroidery, German glass bottles, violins from Prague, Italian carved furniture and marble, Bohemian rock-crystal glassware and American watches.

Another section was devoted to the ingenuity of local workmen who had contributed models in wood, bronze, ebony and paper, e.g. models of the Scott Monument, Melrose Abbey, the Tsar's yacht, a tree-felling Gladstone and a working 'elevator' or lift. One portentous item was a Newhaven joiner's model of a vessel for firing torpedoes at underwater mines.

Unlike the Crystal Palace, the 1886 International Exhibition in Edinburgh was able to remain open to the public after dusk as a result of the installation of electric lighting at a cost of £5,000; 3,200 lamps were lit by power from nine dynamos.

In the north-east corner of the Meadows, Gowans designed and built a Model Cottage of two storeys for four working-class families. He described this sandstone building in another short book, Model Dwelling Houses (1886), and stressed its importance from a social point of view. Gowans's building was awarded by the jurors a diploma of honour 'for suggestiveness and general arrangement in matters affecting light, ventilation, drainage and sanitary appliances'.

Gowans's choice of planning the staircase in the *centre* of the building was based on his desire for plenty of space in the staircase and lobbies and for the maximum amount of light and air; it also allowed each family to have their own entrance. Gowans regarded the staircase in this type of flatted house as the 'lungs' of the building. A large cupola over the staircase ceiling allowed a flood of light, and his belief in the importance of light even led him to incorporate in the upper landing an iron skeletal frame into which were inserted squares of thick rolled glass. This produced the effect of obstructing the view from below of activity on the upper landing for the sake of privacy, but allowing light to fill the ground floor.

Each apartment contained a parlour (9 ft x 7 ft), which could serve as an extra bedroom if required; a bedroom (14 ft x 13 ft) and a lavatory; baths were installed in the upper flats.

Gowans intended after the closure of the exhibition to house local gardeners in this Model Cottage, but an Act of Parliament which forbids all permanent buildings within the Meadows resulted, like the exhibition building itself, in its demolition.

Among the surviving memorials of the 1886 International Exhibition are the two Memorial Masons' Pillars at the north-west entrance to the Meadows and the Prince Albert Victor Sundial. The two octagonal pillars, 26 ft high and surmounted by 7 ft unicorns, were designed by Gowans and built by the Master Builders and Operative Masons of Edinburgh and Leith. They comprise eighteen courses of red, white and yellow sand-stone from seventeen different quarries in Scotland and northern England, the names of which were carved for future comparison as to durability and colouring. On each of the plain faces of the shafts examples were given of masons' marks and masons' work, such as hammer-daubed, nidged, scabbled, splitter-striped and strugged. Twenty-four shields on the caps and centre courses display the Imperial, Scottish, English and Irish arms, the coats of arms of nineteen Scottish burghs and the crest of the Edinburgh masons.

The octagonal sundial in the Meadows was also designed by James Gowans and was adorned by an armillary sphere of bronze, which acted as a sundial. On the fifth course of stone other dials were cut and the lower courses carved with masons' marks and appropriate lines, such as 'Light is the shadow of God', 'Time is the chrysalis of eternity' and 'Man's days are as a shadow that passeth away'. Gowans designed the 13 ft brass column which was cast as the contribution of the Edinburgh and Leith brassfounders; the column was surmounted by a 4½ ft sculpture of a brassworker by J. S. Rhind. This memorial was later moved from the exhibition and used to stand in the garden of Nicolson Square in Edinburgh.

On 18 August 1886, Queen Victoria visited the Edinburgh International Exhibition and the occasion was marked by a Highland Gathering and Games and a series of balloon ascents by intrepid Captain Dale in his gas-filled *Sunbeam*. Before her departure, Queen Victoria knighted James Gowans.

After having been open for six months, the exhibition was closed on 30 October 1886, only after a great public gathering at the Meadows in honour of Sir James Gowans and his family. The event, which had cost £40,000, attracted almost 2½ million visitors and made a profit of £20,000.

However, with the strain of steering through such a vast enterprise and the effect of prostatitis, Gowans's health and finances began to suffer and he was forced to sell Rockville and move to a smaller house nearby in Blantyre Terrace. Gowans's last public engagement took place a month after the official opening of the Forth Bridge in 1890 when he presented a portrait to the Marquis of Lothian on behalf of the exhibition's executive committee. After that occasion, he was unable to leave his house and for more than thirty hours before his death he was unconscious.

Sir James Gowans died in Edinburgh on 25 June 1890 and was buried five days later in the Grange Cemetery.

E

NOTES

1. (Sir) John Summerson, *Architecture in Britain, 1530-1830,* London, 1953, p. 311. The Royal High School in 1968 was forced to desert its magnificent geographical situation for a site outside the city centre. Hamilton's building has since become the City of Edinburgh Art Gallery.

2. Lord Cockburn, *Memorials of his Time,* Edinburgh, 1856; rev. edn., 1945, p. 173. Cockburn's unpublished travel journal is now in the National Library of Scotland.

3. John Ruskin, *Lectures on Architecture and Painting,* delivered at Edinburgh in November 1853, London, 1854, p. 76.

4. Cockburn, op. cit., p. 172.

5. (Sir) James Gowans, *On the Use of Building Stones,* Edinburgh, 1883.

6. Cf. 'Andrew Dalziel used to agree with those who say that it is partly owing to its Presbyterianism that Scotland is less classical than Episcopal England.' Cockburn, op. cit., p. 18.

7. Robert Macleod, *Style and Society: Architectural Ideology in Britain, 1835-1914,* London, 1971, p. 85. See also Duncan McAra, 'The Master-Builders: Essential Art of Scotland', *Scotsman,* 4 March 1972.

8. See John Gage, *Turner:* Rain, Steam and Speed, London, 1972.

9. (Sir) J. H. A. MacDonald, *Life Jottings of an Old Edinburgh Citizen,* Edinburgh, 1915, p. 19.

10. David Bremner, *Industries of Scotland,* Edinburgh, 1869, pp. 412-14.

11. Peter Collins, *Concrete: The Vision of a New Architecture.* London, 1959, p. 27.

12. See J. N. Tarn, *Working-class Housing in 19th-century Britain,* London, 1971, Chapter 7.

13. (Sir) James Gowans, *Royal Commission on the Housing of the Working Classes, Second Report (Scotland),* 1885. p. 27.

14. Ruskin, op. cit., p. 34.
15-22. Gowans, *On the Use of Building Stones.*
23. See C. Gunn, H. Blanc & C. Bedford, *George Heriot's Hospital,* Edinburgh, 1902; the appendix includes three pages of masons' marks on this seventeenth-century building collected by Gowans.
24. Gowans, *On the Use of Building Stones.*
25. From the Reus Museum MS. See E. Casanelles, *Antonio Gaudí: A Reappraisal,* London, 1967, p. 117.
26. James S. Richardson, *The Mediaeval Stone-Carver in Scotland,* Edinburgh, 1964, p. 14.
27. (Sir) John Summerson, *Heavenly Mansions,* London, 1949, p. 158.
28. Summerson, op. cit., p. 141.
29. The demolition of Rockville (while still structurally sound) in January 1966 by James Miller & Partners with the approval of Edinburgh Corporation Town Planning Committee was, in my view, an act of vandalism brought about by visual illiteracy and ignorance of architectural history.
30. (Sir) James Gowans, Paper read to Architectural Institute of Scotland, reprinted in the *Builder,* XVIII, 1860, p. 161.
31. It is interesting to compare Gowans's system with Joseph Gwilt's theory in connection with the Greek Revival. In *The Theory of Proportion in Architecture* (1958), P. H. Scholfield wrote: 'A very different approach to the problem of proportion was made by Gwilt. His own system of planning by means of a grid of squares, borrowed from the French writer Durand, . . . foreshadows much present-day "modular planning".'
32. *Daily Scotsman,* 18 August 1859.
33. Gowans, op. cit., p. 161.
34. *Daily Scotsman,* 18 August 1859.
35-7. Gowans, op. cit., p. 161.
38. N. Taylor, 'Modular Rockery', *Architectural Review,* CXLI, 1967, pp. 147-51.
39. Gowans's first wife, Elizabeth (*née* Mitchell), aged twenty-eight, died in her bath in 1858.
40. Gowans, op. cit., p. 161.
41. *Builder,* XVIII, 1860, p. 161.

42. H. S. Goodhart-Rendel, *How Architecture is Made*, London, 1947, pp. 98-100.

43. See Peter Womersley, 'Approach to Architecture', *RIBA Journal*, LXXVI, 1969, pp. 189-96; also George Perkin (ed.), *Concrete in Architecture*, London, 1968.

44. Gordon Cullen, *Townscape*, London, 1961, p. 92.

45. It is probable that Moxey Sheppard was related to Lammerburn's owner, Francis Sheppard.

46. Bremner, op. cit., pp. 412-14.

47. H. Labouchère, *Report to the Chancellor of the Exchequer regarding the Affairs of the City of Edinburgh and Port of Leith*, Edinburgh, 1836, p. 11.

48. See James Somerville, *Baronial House of Somerville*, Glasgow, 1920.

49. Gowans, op. cit., p. 161.

50. (Sir) John Betjeman, *First and Last Loves*, London, 1952, p. 22. For a trenchant account of recent developments adversely affecting Betjeman's remark, see Colin McWilliam, 'Edinburgh Conserved?' *Architects' Journal*, CLIX, 1974, pp. 109-20.

51. Taylor, op. cit., pp. 147-51.

52. Summerson, op. cit., p. 141.

53. David Walker, *Architects and Architecture in Dundee, 1770-1914*, Dundee, 1955, p. 20. Two unpublished studies of Pilkington's work have been written by Thomas Davies and Hugh Dixon.

54. Discussing the architecture of Antoni Gaudí in *Architecture: Nineteenth and Twentieth Centuries* (1958), Henry-Russell Hitchcock wrote: 'A large suburban villa, built of rubble masonry liberally banded with polychrome tiles, the Casa Vicens passes beyond the extravagances of a Teulon or a Lamb in the sixties into a world of fantasy that only one or two High Victorian designers such as the Scottish Frederick T. Pilkington ever entered.'

55. Colin McWilliam, 'Victorian Architecture: Scotland's Maligned Heritage', *Scotsman*, 26 January 1966.

56. *Builder*, XXVI, 1868, p. 778.

57. *Builder*, XXVII, 1869, p. 623.

58. W. G. Shiells, Paper read to Edinburgh Architectural Association, reprinted in the *Builder*, XXVIII, 1870, pp. 1004-5.

59. D. L. G. Hunter, *Edinburgh's Transport*, Huddersfield, 1964, pp. 18-19.

60. 'One thing in its favour is that Mr Gowans's geometrical details can be executed rapidly.' *Builder*, XXXIII, 1875, p. 569.

61. *Builder*, XXXIII, 1875, pp. 167 and 420.

62. The Synod Hall, demolished in 1966, occupied the site on which will be built Edinburgh's New Royal Lyceum Theatre.

63. D. A. Small, *Through Memory's Window: Edinburgh 1860-1927*, Edinburgh, 1928, p. 9.

64. Gowans, *Royal Commission on the Housing of the Working Classes, Second Report (Scotland)*, 1885, p. 29.

65. (Sir) James Gowans, 'Sanitary Regulations of Buildings', *Transactions*, Edinburgh Meeting, 1880, National Association for the Promotion of Social Science, London, 1881, pp. 529-37.

66-8. (Sir) James Gowans, *The Maintenance of the Health of the People and the Beauty of our City*, Edinburgh, 1885.

69. (Sir) J. J. Burnet studied at the Ecole des Beaux Arts in Paris from 1876 to 1878.

70. Sydney Mitchell was the architect of the picturesque Well Court housing scheme (1884) in Dean Village, Edinburgh.

BIBLIOGRAPHY

Chadwick, G. F., *The Works of Sir Joseph Paxton*, London, 1961.

Collins, Peter, *Changing Ideals in Modern Architecture, 1750-1950*, London, 1965.

Crook, J. Mordaunt, *The Greek Revival: Neo-Classical Attitudes in British Architecture, 1760-1870*, London, 1972.

(Ed.), *Victorian Architecture: A Visual Anthology*, New York, 1971.

Crossland, J. Brian, *Victorian Edinburgh*, Letchworth, 1966.

Dunbar, John G., *The Historic Architecture of Scotland*, London, 1966.

Dyos, H. J., & Wolff, Michael (eds.), *The Victorian City: Images and Realities*, 2 vols., London, 1973.

Edinburgh Architectural Association, *Edinburgh: An Architectural Guide*, Edinburgh, 1964; 2nd edn., 1969.

Edinburgh International Exhibition, *Catalogue of Paintings and other Works of Art*, Edinburgh, 1886.

Official Catalogue, Edinburgh, 1886.

Ferriday, Peter (ed.), *Victorian Architecture*, London, 1963.

Gauldie, Sinclair, *Architecture*, London, 1969.

Germann, Georg, *Gothic Revival in Europe and Britain: Sources, Influences and Ideas*, London, 1972.

Girouard, Mark, *The Victorian Country House*, London, 1971.

Gomme, Andor, & Walker, David, *Architecture of Glasgow*, London, 1968.

Goodhart-Rendel, H. S., *How Architecture is Made*, London, 1947.

'Rogue Architects of the Victorian Era,' *RIBA Journal*, LVI, 1949.

Harvey, John, *The Mediaeval Architect*, London, 1972.

Hay, George, *Architecture of Scotland*, Newcastle, 1969.

Hersey, George L., *High Victorian Gothic: A Study in Associationism*, Baltimore, 1972.

Hitchcock, Henry-Russell, *Early Victorian Architecture in Britain*, 2 vols., New Haven, 1954.
Architecture: Nineteenth and Twentieth Centuries, Harmondsworth, 1958; 3rd edn., 1968.

Howarth, Thomas, *Charles Rennie Mackintosh and the Modern Movement*, London, 1952.

Jordan, Robert F., *Victorian Architecture*, Harmondsworth, 1966.

Kaye, Barrington, *The Development of the Architectural Profession in Britain*, London, 1960.

Kellett, John R., *The Impact of Railways on Victorian Cities*, London, 1969.

Lethaby, W. R., *Philip Webb and his Work*, London, 1935.

Lindsay, Ian, *Georgian Edinburgh*, Edinburgh, 1948; 2nd edn., 1973.

Macleod, Robert, *Charles Rennie Mackintosh*, London, 1968.
Style and Society: Architectural Ideology in Britain, 1835-1914, London, 1971.

Matthew, (Sir) Robert, Reid, John & Lindsay, Maurice (eds.), *The Conservation of Georgian Edinburgh*, Edinburgh, 1972.

Minto, C. S., *Victorian and Edwardian Edinburgh from Old Photographs*, London, 1973.

Muthesius, Stefan, *The High Victorian Movement in Architecture, 1850-1870*, London, 1972.

Pevsner, (Sir) Nikolaus, *An Outline of European Architecture*, Harmondsworth, 7th edn., 1963.
Pioneers of Modern Design, Harmondsworth, 3rd edn., 1960.
Ruskin and Viollet-le-Duc, London, 1969.

Richardson, James S., *The Mediaeval Stone-Carver in Scotland*, Edinburgh, 1964.

Rolt, L. T. C., *Thomas Telford*, London, 1958.

Ruskin, John, *The Seven Lamps of Architecture*, London, 1849.
The Stones of Venice, 3 vols., London, 1851-3.

Scholfield, P. H., *The Theory of Proportion in Architecture*, Cambridge, 1958.

Scully, Vincent, *The Shingle Style and the Stick Style*, New Haven, 1955; 2nd edn., 1971.

Service, Alastair (ed.) *Edwardian Architecture and its Origins*, London, 1975.

Stanton, Phoebe, *Pugin*, London, 1971.

Summerson, (Sir) John, *Heavenly Mansions*, London, 1949. *Victorian Architecture: Four Studies in Evaluation*, New York, 1970.

Tarn, J. N., *Working-class Housing in 19th-century Britain*, London, 1971.

Thompson, Paul, *William Butterfield*, London, 1971.

Walker, David, *Architects and Architecture in Dundee, 1770-1914*, Dundee, 1955.

West, Thomas, *A History of Architecture in Scotland*, London, 1967.

Young, Andrew McLaren, & Doak, A. M. (eds.), *Glasgow at a Glance*, Glasgow, 1965; 2nd edn., 1971.

Youngson, A. J., *The Making of Classical Edinburgh*, Edinburgh, 1966.

INDEX

Sir James Gowans.

Rosebank Cottages, Edinburgh (1854-5): one
of several pioneering working-class housing
schemes in the city.

Redhall Bank Cottages, Edinburgh (1857).

Rockville, 3 Napier Road, Edinburgh (1858): a contemporary
engraving from the "Builder" (1860).

Rockville: demolished in 1966.

Rockville: view from a window of Lammerburn.

Rockville: rear elevation, including bas-relief on right of Gowans.

Rockville: bas-relief of Sir James Gowans by William Brodie, RSA. Note the geometric plans, books and pair of compasses — all carved from stone.

Rockville: detail of chimney masonry.

Rockville: vividly painted ground-floor window with intertwining Gs and bordered by gowans (Scots for wild daisies).

Rockville: detail of a leg of the garden table, decorated with gowans.

The Lodge (1858): a brilliant example of disciplined draughtsman-
ship and geometric precision.

The Lodge, with Rockville in the foreground.

Lammerburn, 10 Napier Road, Edinburgh (1859).

23 and 25 Blacket Place, Edinburgh (1860-1).

Lochee Station, Dundee (1861).

Farm-labourer's cottage, Gowanbank, West Lothian (1862).

Cottage for the clerk of Redhall Quarry, Edinburgh (c. 1863). Nearby stand the earlier cottages of 1857.

25-36 Castle Terrace, Edinburgh (1866-70).

New Edinburgh Theatre, Castle Terrace, Edinburgh (1875). In 1877 it was altered to become the Synod Hall. Demolished in 1966 to make room for a new theatre and opera house.

The twin crown-capped towers of 27 Castle Terrace, Edinburgh.

'Suggested Improvement of the North Bridge': 26 in x 52 in pen and ink drawing with colour wash; in bottom right corner is the signature 'James Gowans, Archt. 1870'. This drawing, first shown in the 1870 RSA Exhibition, is now on display in Huntly House Museum, Canongate, Edinburgh.